Perceived Thoughts

Shauna Cesar

DEDICATION

This book is dedicated to my love, my husband, Andrew for believing in me and giving me the time and support to follow my dreams. Also my family and friends who have encouraged me to write and be myself no matter what.

CONTENTS

INTRODUCTION

Welcome to my brain part two. In this installment I have continued the honesty and hopefully openness. The title Perceived Thoughts has double meaning to me as all poems fit into one of two categories; how I perceive people that have crossed my life's path, and my form of poetic ways to describe thoughts and feelings I have had throughout my life.

Shauna Cesar

PERCEIVED

Lies

My heart is drenched in lies
So heavy and full
Close to its breaking point
I've lost my heart and soul

I gave you all my trust
And you ate it up
Filling my head with stories
My soul being snuck away

Don't put your blame on me
You pulled all the strings
Had me dancing like a puppet
For your joy and entertainment

You think you have all the answers
To keep me playing your game
Stuck in the dark oblivious
No longer content in your lies

Colors

Your shirt was green
When we first met

The sky was blue
On our first date

My dress was purple
First time you left

Lights danced green
When we fell in love

The walls were cream
In our first place

The world felt grey
On our last day

Your soul showed black
With things you said

My vision was red
When we parted

Open Eyes

What did you think would happen
When you ran away
I felt like I was ripped open
Bare to the toxic air
Our time together
Playing through my mind

What did you think would happen
When you showed up
Returning with smooth words
And the shining smile
My pain dismissed
Refusing to acknowledge it

What did you think had happened
While you were gone
Forever disillusioned to your game
Eroded bear soul
Tiny heart pieces
Foggy brain wishing your return

What did you think would happen
I'd forget the pain
You'd play with my heart
Never happening again

You

I hear you whispering
I love you
As I turn and walk away

Disregarding all that's said
I need you
But I continue anyway

Making my way gone
I'll make it
Trying to stay away

Knowing it is no use
I crave you
Not caring if it hurts

Returning to you
I miss you
But it's not the same

The illusion has been shattered
I move on
Never to return again

Jasmine

A window to eternity
Where all is healed
Blocked by a smile
So sickly sweet
Surrounding darkness
That never ends
Promises of happiness
Without a word spoke
If only the fog
Gets parted
Tossed here and there
On a turbulent sea
Amidst the waves
Threatening to sink
All goodness within
Handed lemons and rocks
Becoming bruised and broken
From the inside
Emerging from the storm
Never to be the same

Beautiful

What a beautiful creature
Belonging to no one
Backlit by the full moon
Oblivious to my longing

To be that free
Accepted and desired
I just want a taste
Of your sweet perfection

The friendship that grows
With a beautiful creature
Nurtures my soul
Makes me feel good

Perfection permeates me
You taste so sweet
I'm instantly addicted
Your crazy masked

Fond memories forever
Of a beautiful creature
Belonging to no one
Not so oblivious

Thinking

I think of you day and night
Wish for your body next to mine
You gave me a glimpse
Of the possibility
Of bliss

I think of you night and day
Of all the things
You used to say
Promises never made
Futures designed

I think of you day and night
You played a game
With my heart and mind
You played them well
You won

PERCEIVED THOUGHTS

I think of you night and day
Of smiles and secrets
Just you and me
The rain and park
Forever changed

I think of you day and night
A little less every day
No more tears
For futures designed
Or you

Trampled

For all I know this
Is where I belong
Crumpled on the floor
Broken from the inside

No one is around
To pick me up
The weight of the world
Holding me down

Everything taken away
With one quick action
You walked away
And I fell down

Sick with shame
My stomach rolls
Look what I've come to
You took my self

No more strength
Or so you tried
I will return
But in how long

Without

Your constant lust
For things you don't have
Repulses me

The inevitable want
For selfish pursuits
Enrages me

Living your life
A constant want for more
Saddens me

My life being whole
Not consumed by want
Encourages me

Without your presence
In my daily life forever
Relieves me

The Crowd

Wild eyes
Naked soul
Vast void
Broken heart

Weary eyes
Tired soul
Slumped shoulders
Large heart

Soft eyes
Open soul
Quick embrace
Warm heart

Wicked eyes
Evil soul
Fake smile
Black heart

Dull eyes
Quiet soul
Broken faith
Dying heart

Goodbye

I said goodbye
To you last night
In my dream

I saw tears form
As you frowned
When I walked away

I've held on
For too long
Not sure if you care

Even my dreams
Say it's time
To move on

Clear my heart
No more longing
Farewell my dear

Narcissist

My life is a battle
I fight and win
To make it this far
Is my accomplishment

What's mine
Stays mine
No one to say
Any different

No one takes it
No one leaves
Unless I allow it
All will is mine

If you want it
Come get it
Try to take it from me
See what happens

Empty

He's dead
I can feel it
There's nothing left
Of his soul

Looking alive
From the outside
An empty shell
Of a man

He smiles
I can see it
There's no light
In his eyes

The outside
May look good
There's rotten within
Life long gone

Escape

Clingy and needy
Surrounding me
Need some freedom
To spread my wings

Stunted growth
Feeling the shade
Straight to my soul
Suffocating inside

Not feeling right
No clear escape
It wasn't supposed to
Be this way

Freedom and acceptance
Are promises broken
Put in a box
Expected to stay

I will fail
Or suffocate
Losing my sanity
To please you

Worse Than Others

Who were you to judge me
When sharing my feelings
Stealing my inner thoughts
And making them your own

You claimed to move past
But still clinging to it
Time has not dulled the pain
And yet it has blurred the details

Everything I do is subject to judgement
Scrutinized by your eyes
Nothing will be good enough
I can't make you happy

If I leave you alone
You say you will be lost
But I can't live in constant alert
Worried you will misinterpret

The manipulation of my brain
My feelings and thoughts
Makes you worse than others
I've already left behind

Spreading cold

If you love me
Never let me go
Treat me right
Show me off

If you play games
Leave me be
Move along
Save your breath

My precious heart
And sweet soul
Can take no more
Slowly fading away

Your sparkle eyes
Breathtaking smile
Hide it good
Stone cold heart

Never again
A pile of broken
Your stone cold
Is spreading

Self-Loathing

Celebrate a decaying dark
Secretly smile and desire
A haunting embrace

Once full of warmth
Devour or die
Kissing to conquer

Poisoned by life
The sour circumstances
Of surviving

Living each day
To ruin another's
 Celebrating evil spread

If I'm in darkness
Everything I touch
Joins me

Outside is deceiving
Happiness and sunshine
Hiding all else

Happy

I wanted it
So bad
I worked it
So hard
Why did it
Fail

I gave up
So sad
I picked up
So fast
Better things were
Coming

I dreamed you
So long
I loved you
So much
You make me
Happy

Salvation

Almost hard to breathe
With brilliant fire melting
A cold prisoner
Of dark times

Like slipping into a dream
After a long tiring day
An escapee
With fleeting freedom

To make full use
Of time in the sun
Exuberant energy burning
Quickly threw my shell

Still I find salvation
In the look in your eyes
The acceptance
Of all of me

Want

All I want is him
My love can wait
No more

The feeling of being
In his embrace
So safe

All I want is us
My love returned
And whole

The feeling of trust
And true happiness
So pure

All I want is this
My love and me
No others

The feeling of whole
Body and soul
Forever

My Love

Your language so smooth
It calmed the sea
Choppy and churning
Inside of me

The shadows cry
Trying to return
Banished in exile
From your light

Beneath the surface
My crazy peeks through
Threatening to ruin
Our good thing

Through my frantic panic
You still calm me
And sooth my soul
Our love prevails

Shauna Cesar

THOUGHTS

Winter

Quick push
Into the depths
Frantic life
Embrace it fully
Smell Spring
Paces are slowing
Less hectic
As life relaxes
Together yet
So far apart
Mad ache
For one another
Never resting
Until we're whole

A Ship

Drifting along
Like fog over water
No known destination
Lost

Only you
Hold the anchor line
Pull and drag me
Back

Ground me
And bring me home
Before I become
Undone

Twenty

I asked an angel
For a kiss of life
To heal my heart
From my liquid death

The glass half full
Of clear poison
Drinking away the pain
That is my whole life

I asked the universe
To take me away
From my pain
And dark foggy mind

Days blurring to night
Memories getting foggy
Forgetting myself
Unbearable disappointment

I ask the unknown
For a glimmer of hope
Something to turn around
My impending doom

Grown-up

Shadows in the mist
Take a scary form
Crushing the sweet ideals
Whispering the ugly truths

Playing dress-up in a
Grown-up world
Bitter from the symphony
Of surrounding judgements

Trudging through the days
Languid and emotionless
Bitter from the staleness
Of monotonous existence

Shadows creep closer
Forms more defined
Threatening to take over
And mix life up

Needing something new
Before life breaks
Can't put the pieces
Together over and over

Addiction

A light storm
Flying above me

Lazy water
Flowing beneath

There's a crushing blow
From the shadows

Full of ugly wants
Of more than sleep

All hope is gone
Of tonight being different

The urgent need
Completely takes over

When addiction
Runs your life

Morning After

Bright lights
They hurt

Loud noise
It pounds

Four walls
Are spinning

My stomach
Is churning

Standing not
An option

Rolling off
The bed

Crawling across
The floor

Promises of
Never again

Quitting

Tiny bitter urges
Pounding need
Dream of relief

Pure dark soul
Twisted want
Must not cave

Looks so good
Crushing need
Smells of heaven

Easy to find
Urgent want
Must not go

Slow calm breath
Waning need
Time has passed

Leave it alone
Vanishing want
Need no more

Coffee

Frantic whisper
Panting cry
Soul aches

Luscious lips
Heaving chest
Enormous urges

Hot breath
Smooth words
Dripping fast

Sweet shine
Into clouds
Raw heat

Blow softly
Closed eyes
Quiet worship

Tiny sigh
Small sips
Cravings replete

Push

Elaborate dreams are broken
Revealing shadowed thoughts
Pushing me away
From lofty goals and wants

Now that I know what I'm missing
Can I push to get it back
Change my course
To a life full of potential

Self-doubt and uncertainty
Push themselves forward
Front and center
Not content kept in the dark

With love and support
I can keep moving forward
Push past doubt
Put my dreams back together

Freedom

Lying in an ocean
Of cool grass
A prisoner of here

Frozen voiced and
Surrounded in dark
Waking slowly to life

Breaking through the cold
To embrace myself
Accepting all that is now

Sparkling skies engross
An open mind
No longer a prisoner

Thoughts of my own
Rushing the brain
For the first time remembered

Cool breeze tickles my
Goose bumped skin
Freedom feels good

Watch me

I'm only human
Watch me fail
But I always
Try again

I'm only human
Watch me fall
And pick myself
Back up

I'm only human
Watch me cry
Falling to pieces
Temporary pain

I'm only human
Watch me love
No holding back
Whole hearted

I'm only human
Watch me live
A bright future
Straight ahead

Struggles

Who knew
It physically hurts
To be mentally
Exhausted

Who knew
Imaginary slights
Could cause such
Sadness

Who knew
Not being able to
Keep focus would
Alienate

Who knew
I would find
A few people to
Stay

The Cycle

When the urge hits
And emotion is raw
The hearts whispers no
As the fog sets in

Sleep now eludes
And energy is high
Watch the moon change
as the days blur

Some day soon
My body will tire
And heart will pound
As the crash comes

When the body exhausts
Thoughts will race
And the brain's still wired
As the dark engulfs

Looking for a plain
Even and true
Need less up and down
And sanity to return

Paranoia

A ghost from the past
With ferocious
All seeing eyes

Once a peaceful prisoner
Of an empty
Haunted smile

Surveying what damage
Can be done with
Devious mind

Often ruining the good
Once revealed
In the open

Trying to hold it back
A fruitless effort
Once released

The end is nearer
Each passing moment
Paranoia spreads

Bleak Clouds

Darkness climbed in
Clouding a beautiful life
Peace and harmony never thrive
Shade growing roots
Feeling blue
Withers the spirit

Happiness brings rays
Of sunshine and hope
Breaking through
Depressive clouds
For brief moments

Bleak and grey
Becoming the new normal
Sucking all enjoyment
From life's moments

Happiness fights to stay
Valent efforts are denied
Hope forever dimmed

All happiness gone
Living life in black and grey

Battered and Torn

Living a life
Of rain and storms
Hard to catch my breath

With the wind blowing
A frantic beat
Feeling battered and torn

Struggling to wait out
The rain and storm
To live a calmer life

Cuts

Asked about the blood
I lie and play it off
Wanting to please you
Raw with emotion
The smell on my skin
Sickly sweet
The air tastes metallic
I don't know how
To ask for help

Asked about the scars
I don't know the answer
Wanting to explain
An unwanted response
To an unknown
Inner battle
The easiest way
To let it out
Is releasing the pressure

Demons

Dreams full of raw emotion
Whispering urges seeping through
Wishing reality was calm and smooth

Deception and lies abound
Making love ugly and worn
Truth is blurry from so far away

Determined to turn things around
Living life good and honest
Getting through the days

Denying the pressing urges
Fighting natural demons
Is this what happiness looks like

On Auto

Feeling tired
Need some comfort
Catching teardrops
On my shirt

Sleepless night
My empty bed
Sick and tired
Feeling lonely

Dreary day
Stuck on auto
Like a puppet
On a string

Never ending
Living a loop
Has no beginning
See no end

Kindred soul
Life picks up
Sharing the days
Comfort at night

Lost Within

Swimming through a sea
Of hazy dreams
Trying to reach
The surface

Lost within the waves
Panic setting in
No visible end
In sight

Distant reality is fading
Scenes in black and white
I'm a danger
To myself

Why can't I wake up
Shake off this haze
Start to live
My life

Bipolar

I am tired
Of being left behind
Passed over
Forgotten

I am anxious
Of new situations
New places
People

It's not contagious
My worries and stress
My sadness
Exhaustion

All in my head
This troubling disease
My disorder
Bipolar

ABOUT THE AUTHOR

Shauna Cesar is the author of Three Die Divination and the poetry collection Enter My Mind. Shauna lives in Calgary, Alberta with her husband and children. She is a self-proclaimed nerd who loves to read and write.